I0201901

The Mystery of the Lost Tribes of Israel
Unveiled

and
A Brief Study of the Eons

EDMUND 'CLARK' TRAVIS

Copyright © 2023 – Edmund 'Clark' Travis
All cover art copyright © – Edmund 'Clark' Travis
All Rights Reserved

No part of this book may be reproduced or transmitted in any form or by any means, electronic or mechanical, including photocopying, recording, or by any information storage and retrieval system, without permission in writing from the author.

INDIE
PUB
PRESS
Independently Published

ISBN -13: 978-1-960499-68-4

DEDICATION

It is my desire to dedicate this work to my wife, Marilyn June, of almost 65 years. We married on June 17, 1950, and she passed away on March 28, 2015. She is missed by many.

In addition, I want to remember some friends with whom we enjoyed Bible study on Friday evenings for several years. Elwood and Jackie Gustafson, Jack and Connie Rahn, and of course, Marilyn. They have all passed away, but I still have fond memories of those good times.

All quotations are from the Condordant bible. All bracketed words are placed there by me. All italicized words are for emphasis by me.

TABLE OF CONTENTS

THE MYSTERY
OF THE LOST TRIBES
UNVEILED

It has been said, the law of grace can be found in the Old Testament Scriptures, but God has kept the truth from being divulged to the people. That is certainly true of the restoration of the cast away tribes of Israel, for there, is revealed the complete process, from being cast way to being regathered in the land of Canaan. Furthermore, the process is repeated in the New Testament, but God has kept the truth from being known until these times.

The Ten Tribes Cast Away

Some history of Israel should be of help in beginning this study. In about 808 BC the ten tribes became so wicked, by following the Gentile way of life, that God separated them from the other two, Judah and Benjamin. The ten tribes retained the name, Israel, while the two tribes took the name Judah. In 611 BC Israel had continued their wickedness to the point God cast them away. At that time the two tribes regained the name, Israel, which they retain to this day.

"For I will not continue further to have compassion on the house of Israel. Yet on the house of Judah, I will have compassion, and I will save them by Ieue their Alueim, yet I will not save them by bow or by sword or by battle, by horses or by horsemen." (Hos. 1:6B-7). "Yet the number of the sons of Israel shall number as the sand of the sea, which is not being measured or numbered.

And it comes to be in the place in which it was being said to them, Not My people are you. There shall it be said to them, sons of the living Al. And the sons of Judah and the sons of Israel shall be convened together." (Hos. 1:10-11A).

We gain further insight from words of the prophets, which shall be quoted here. Hosea speaks of the day of this gathering.

"Go, and we will return to Ieue our
  Alueim.
For He tore to pieces, and He will heal
us: He was smiting, and He will bind us
  up.
He will make us alive after two days:
In the third day He will raise us up,
And we shall live before Him."
  (Hos. 6:1-2).

Amos also speaks of the day Ephraim shall be restored. **(Note! We shall learn more about the title of Ephraim later.)** Amos spoke the following words more than seventy-five years before the house of Israel was cast away.

"Behold! The eyes of my Lord Ieue
  are on the sinning kingdom,
And I will exterminate it off the surface
  of the ground,
Only that I will not utterly exterminate
  the house of Jacob, (averring is Ieue).
For behold! I am instructing,
And I will jerk the house of Israel to and
  fro among the nations.
Just as grain in a sieve is jerked to and fro,
And I will exterminate it off the surface of
  the ground,
Yet a pouchful shall not fall to the earth."
  (Amos 9:8-9).

Even as Ephraim has been tossed about among the Gentile nations, but not a pouchful shall be lost, their salvation will be total, and their faith shall reveal Christ Jesus to the people.

Zephaniah has the following to say about 4the limping remnant, which is Ephraim.

"Behold! Me dealing with all those
  humbling you,
    at that season, (averring is Ieue).
And I will save her who is limping,
And her which is expelled, I will convene,

And I will make them a praise and a
  lname,
In the entire earth of their shame.
In that season I will bring you in,
Even at the season of My convening you;
For I will give you a name and a praise
  among all the peoples of the earth,
In My reversal of your captivities
  before your eyes, says Ieue."
  (Zeph. 3:19-20).

Zechariah prophesied one hundred years
before the tribes were cast away. Yet he says
the following about them through Ephraim.
Not only does he speak of their restoration,
he says a special place must be provided, for
there is no room for them.

"And the house of Joseph will I save.
And I will cause them to dwell,
For I have compassion on them,
And they shall come to be
As if I had not cast them off:
For I am Ieue their Alueim,
And I respond to them.
And Ephraim shall become as a master,
And their heart shall rejoice as from wine,
And their sons shall see, and they shall

rejoice.
Their heart shall exult in Ieue.
I shall hiss for them and convene them.
For I ransom them, and they increase,
  just as they have increased.
And I will sow them among the peoples,
Yet in the far places they shall
  remember Me.
And they shall live with their sons and
  return.
And I restore them from the land of
  Egypt,
And from Assyria will I convene them.
And to the land of Gilead and Lebanon
  will I bring them,
Yet no room will be found for them."
(Zech. 10:6-10).

Indeed, a place will be needed for them to assemble. Seven areas of Asia Minor will be prepared for them, and at their resurrection, they, then called Ephraim, shall go there to dwell through the last half of the tribulation period.

Note:! A. E. Knoch, translator of the Hebrew Scriptures into the English Concordant Bible Version, gives four

different titles for God. Al is used about 200 times, and refers to the spirit of God only. Ieue (will-be-ing-was) is used nearly 300 times and refers to His image only. Alue refers to the spirit and the image together, but as one God, only 50 times. Alueim is used over 2000 times and also refers to God as both spirit and image together. Of course, these terms are found only in the Old Testament. I trust this is a good explanation for such a complex matter.

First Mention: Salvation of All

Abram has just heard that his brother's son, Lot, has been captured. Abram gathers three hundred and eighty dedicated ones of his household to fall upon the enemy by night. They restore all his people and their goods and all the goods of Sodom.

After smiting Chedorlaomer, and his kings with him, he meets with the king of Salem. Melchizedek, king of Salem, brings bread and wine. He is priest for Al Supreme,

Owner of the heavens and earth, and "Blessed is the Al Supreme Who awards your foes into your hands." (Gen. 14:21).

And saying is Abram to the king of Sodom, "High hold I my hand to swear to Ieue the Al Supreme, Owner of the heavens and earth, if it is more than a thread or even a sandal lacing, or if taking am I anything which is yours, then will you not say, I enrich Abram? (Gen. 14:22-23).

After these matters the word [Jesus] of Ieue in a vision, came to Abram saying, "You must not fear Abram! I am your shield, your exceedingly increased Hire." (Gen.15:1).

Abram is puzzled, for the one running about his home is not his heir. "Behold! To me no seed have you given and behold! A son of my household is to enjoy my tenancy?" (Gen.15:3).

Then the word [Jesus] of Ieue came to him again, saying, "Not this one is to enjoy your tenancy, but rather one who shall fare forth from your bowels, he is to enjoy your tenancy." (Gen. 15:4).

The word [Jesus] of Ieue brings Abram outside, saying, "Look pray, toward the heavens and number the stars, if you can number them." And saying is He to Abram, "Thus shall your seed become." (Gen. 15:5).

"Abram believes in Ieue Alueim, and reckoning it is He to him for righteousness." (Gen. 15:6).

Note: When we consider the truth that if it were possible for Abram to count the number of stars in the heavens, he would know the number of the seed of Abraham, and then consider the words of Jesus in the vision that He is Abraham's exceedingly *increased* Hire, it must be evident that His death, burial and resurrection brings the seed of Abraham far beyond seeds made up of his natural descendants. I am confident Jesus has assured us of the salvation of all humanity.

God Probes Abraham Concerning His Faith

Because of contention between Abraham's and Lot's graziers, Abram gave Lot his choice of taking all the land to the right or to the left. Lot chose all the basin of the Jordan River, while Abram retained the land of Canaan.

Now Abram's name has been changed to Abraham. The Alueim tells Abraham to take his son Isaac to the land of Moriah and offer his son for an ascent offering on a mountain He would direct him to. Taking two of the lads of his household with him and Isaac, and wood for the ascent offering, they proceeded to the place that Alueim told him about.

Leaving the two lads, Abraham took Isaac and wood for the fire for the offering and placed the wood on his son, and taking in hand the fire and the knife, the two went on together. Reaching the place shown to them, Abraham built an altar and arranged the wood. He trussed Isaac, his son, and placed him on the altar above the wood. Stretching out is Abraham his hand and is taking the knife to slay his son.

And calling is the messenger of Ieue to him from the heavens and saying, "Abraham! Abraham! You must not stretch out your hand upon the lad, and you must not do ought to him, for now I know that you fear the Alueim, for you have not kept back your son, your only one from Me." (Gen. 22:12).

And calling is the messenger of Ieue to Abraham a second time from the heavens, and saying, "By Myself I swear, averring is Ieue, that because you have done this thing and have not kept back your son, your only one, from Me, that, blessing, yea, blessing you am I, and increasing, yea, increasing your seed am I as the stars of the heavens and as the sand of the sea shore. And your seed shall tenant the gateway of its enemies, *and blessed in your seed, shall be all the nations of the earth,* in as much as you hearken to My voice." (Gen. 22:16-18).

Note! While this quotation states that Abraham's seed shall increase as the stars of the heavens and as the sand of the seashore, it seems to have a different connotation than the usage at Gen. 15:6. This seems to indicate only that both are far too many to count, while the usage at Gen. 15:6 implies the count is equal. In addition, we read that all the nations of the earth will be blessed.

Jacob's Secret (Gen. Chapter 48)

Joseph was told that his father was ill. Taking his two sons, Manasseh and Ephraim, he goes to Jacob. Jacob was told that his son is coming to him. Jacob tells Joseph that the One Who Suffices, [Jesus] once appeared to him in Luz, in the land of Canaan, and blessed him. He is to be fruitful and be given an assembly of people as his seed after him, and an eonian freehold. Jacob tells Joseph that Joseph's sons, Manasseh and Ephraim, are to become his. Just as Reuben and Simon are his according to the Covenant of Moses, so Manasseh and Ephraim are his according to the New Covenant of grace.

Jacob's eyes were heavy with age, and he could hardly see, so Joseph brought his sons close. Jacob took the two of them to himself, Manasseh on his left and Ephraim on his right. When Joseph sees his father place his right hand upon Ephraim's head, he attempts to take his hand away. "Not so, my father, for this is the firstborn. Place your right hand upon his head." (Gen. 48:18).

Refusing is his father and saying, "I know

my son! I know! Moreover, he shall become a people, and he shall become great. Howbeit, his smaller brother shall be greater than he. And his seed shall become a fullness of the nations." (Gen. 48:19).

And blessing them is he that day, saying, "The Alueim makes you as Ephraim and Manasseh!" (Gen. 48:20). And placing is he Ephraim before Manasseh.

The greater blessing went to the younger son, Ephraim. The lesser blessing went to the older son, Manasseh. From the time Ephraim was cast away, it was Manasseh that enjoyed the greater blessing. They were considered the greater, though the Alueim would no longer fight their battles. They continued to have His compassion. They were considered the "Circumcision," requiring works such as circumcising all male children on their eighth day after birth. They were Alueim's workmanship, yet He gave them faith to carry out the works. Alueim's faith was the propitiatory shelter until the resurrection of Christ. At the same time, Ephraim was no longer the Alueim's people and received no compassion.

After the resurrection of Christ, Manasseh

continued as the "Circumcision," while Ephraim was being saved by grace, not requiring circumcision and being baptized by the holy spirit.

The name Ephraim is used several times in the Scriptures as the ones that were lost, however, to my knowledge, the two tribes were never called Manasseh. I assume it was because, if that had been recognized, it would no longer be a secret.

Moses visits with Ieue (Ex. 33:12-23)

Moses came down from the mountain after spending time with Ieue and found how the people had betrayed Him with their idol as their god. Moses sought favor from Ieue. He said to Him, "You have said: I know you by name and, moreover, You have found grace in my eyes. And now, I pray, if I have found grace in Your eyes, let me know Your way that I may know You and that I may have grace in Your eyes, to see that this nation is Your people." (Ex. 33:13-14). Ieue said to Moses, "My presence shall it go with you that it may give you rest." (Ex.33:14). Ieue told Moses what he asked He will do, for He found grace in Moses's eyes, and He knows him by name.

He chose a place by Him, where Moses would be stationed on a rock. Then Ieue passed before him, while *He overshadowed His glory with His hand.* This will become significant.

Isaiah's Vision (Isa. 6:1-10)

Isaiah was shown Ieue sitting on a throne in a vision. Seraphim stood above having six wings each, two covering each one's face, two covering its feet, and two for flying. The house is filling with smoke. Isaiah is frightened for he is a man of unclean lips. He had seen Ieue Himself in a vision. One of the seraphim flies to him, and in his hand is a glowing coal. With snuffers, he takes it from the altar.

He is touching Isaiah's lips and "Behold! This touches your lips and withdrawn is your depravity, and for your sins there is a propitiatory shelter." (Isa. 6:7). Isaiah hears the Lord saying, "Whom shall I send?" And Isaiah says, "Behold me! Send me!" (Isa. 6:8). And He is saying to Isaiah,

"Go and say to this people:

Hear ye to hear, yet you must not be understanding.

And see ye to see, yet you must not be knowing.

Stouten the heart of this people,

And their ears make heavy,

And their eyes make squint,

Lest they are seeing with their eyes,

And with their ears are hearing,

And with their heart are understanding,

And turning back, then healing is theirs."

(Isa. 6:9-10).

Israel Restored to the Land

When we read this forty ninth chapter of Isaiah it becomes apparent why God did not want the people to comprehend the meaning. This chapter reveals the role Paul would carry out some six hundred and thirty years into the future.

The 49th chapter of Isaiah describes the regathering of the two houses quite well. The first thirteen verses relate to the return to the land by (Ephraim) the ten tribes, while the last thirteen verses relate to the return of (Manasseh) the two tribes. They will become one nation once again.

Isa. 49:1-13. It was [Paul] that was hidden in the shadow of the hand of Ieue, and [Paul] was the glory that Ieue was concealing from Moses, for he would become representative of all Israel. Ieue is saying, "My servant are you [Paul] in whom I am beautifying Myself." (Isa. 49:3). He [Paul] became weary and feels his labor is for naught. But he knows his judgement is in the hands of his Alueim. This one [Paul] knows he was formed from the belly to be His servant, to restore Jacob when Israel is being restored. "Yet I shall be glorified in the eyes of Ieue and the Alueim becomes my help." (Isa. 49:5).

These are the tribes that were scattered throughout the earth. They are millions and millions, probably billions, of coastlanders and folkstems from afar. It is in [Paul] that Ieue is beautifying Himself. He constitutes

[Paul's] mouth as a sharp sword, and in the shadow of His hand He hides His glory.

Many may argue it must have been Jesus that came to restore the two houses of Israel. Jesus came here to save the world from their sins. He came here to live a sinless life for a world of people that could not accomplish that for themselves. He lived the sinless life, then gave His life on Calvary cross. Because He was sinless, the Alueim raised Him from the tomb to sit on a throne at His Own right hand in the heavens. This was the greatest blessing this world has ever received. But it was Paul who was called to restore the two houses.

"And now," thus said Ieue, "Who formed me [Paul] from the belly for His servant, to restore Jacob to Him when Israel is being gathered to Him. Yet I shall be glorified in the eyes of Ieue and my Alueim becomes my help." (Isa. 49:5).

And He is saying to me, "A slight thing is it for you to become My servant, to raise up the tribes of Jacob, and the dispersed of Israel to restore. Behold! I give you also for a light to the nations, to become My salvation unto the ends of the earth." (Isa.

49:6).

"Thus says my Lord Ieue, your Redeemer, the Alueim of Israel, to the holy One, to the despised of His soul, to the abhorred of the nations, to the servant of rulers. Kings shall see him, and they rise, and chiefs also worship him, on account of Ieue Who is faithful, the Holy One of Israel. And He shall choose you [Paul]." (Isa. 49:7).

"Thus says my Ieue, "In a *season acceptable,* I answer you. And in a day of salvation, I help you. And I will preserve you, and I give you for a covenant of the people, to set up the land, to allot the desolated allotments, to say to those bound, fare forth, and to those in darkness, be revealed! And on all their mountains shall they graze. And all ridges shall be their pasture. They shall not hunger nor thirst, nor will the searing wind and the sun smite them. For the One showing them compassion will lead them, and to fonts of water will He conduct them. And I make ways on all My mountains, and My mountains are high." (Isa. 49:8-11).

The land is filling up with the people who were once lost to the far corners of the earth.

"Behold! These from afar are coming. And behold! These from the north and from the sea, and these from the land of the Sinim. Jubilate, O heavens! And exult, O earth! Crash O mountains, into jubilation! And the hills into righteousness! For the Lord is comforting His people, and on His humble is He having compassion." (Isa. 49:12-13).

(Isa. 49:14-26). The last thirteen verses reveal the two tribes or Manasseh, being restored to the land. "Will a woman forget her child, not to have compassion on the son of her belly? Even if these, a woman will forget, yet I will not forget you, says Ieue, Behold! On My palms I tattoo you, and your walls are in front of Me continually." (Isa. 49:15-16).

Now those who made them a desert are fleeing from them. If they will just look around, they will see who is convened and coming to them. Ieue is with them, and they shall be as clothed with ornament, and they shall tie them on as a bride her wreath. The Gentile nations are their desolations, and the land of their demolitions, but now they are constricted because of the dweller (Ephraim), yet far away are those who swallowed them up.

"Further, the sons of their bereavements [ones taken away] shall say in your ears, constricted for me is the place. Come close to me and I will dwell. And you say in your heart, who generated these for me while I was bereaved and a widow, and deported and withdrawn? And these, who brought them up for me? Behold I remained alone. Yet these, whereat were they? For thus says my Lord, Behold! I will lift My hand to the nations, [Gentiles] and to the people [Gentiles] will I raise My banner high. And they bring your sons in a bosom pouch, and your daughters on their shoulders, shall be borne, and kings become your foster fathers, and their chiefesses your wet nurses. Nostrils to the earth, shall they prostrate to you, and the soil at your feet shall they lick up."(Isa. 49:20:23).

The Beginning of the Body of Christ

The people of Jerusalem have just returned from their captivity in Babylon after seventy years. Remember that Ephraim (the ten tribes) have been cast away, therefore are not part of Israel's return. Joshua is the great priest, but he has become clothed in filthy garments and stands before the messenger. The messenger is saying to those before him, "Take away the filthy garments from off him." (Zech. 3:4). They placed a new turban on his head and clothed him in garments, and Ieue is standing by. The messenger testifies to Joshua, saying, "Thus says Ieue of hosts: should you be going in My ways and should you be keeping My charge, then, moreover, you shall adjudicate over My house and moreover, you shall keep My courts, and I will give you walks between those who are standing by. Hear, pray, Joshua, the great priest, you and your associates who are sitting before you, for *mortals of a miracle* are they, for behold Me bringing in My servant, the Sprout." (Zech. 3:7-8). The Sprout is Jesus. These people are called *symbols of things to come* in the NIV. They are coming to be members of the body of Christ. The italics are mine for emphasis.

Paul writes about these saints in the book of Hebrews. This is from Heb. 12:18-24. He tells of how terrible it was in Moses' days, when the Israelites made the golden idol, while Moses was on the mountain. The mountain was set ablaze and there was murkiness and gloom and tornado, and blare of trumpets, and no word was added to them because the people did not do as they were supposed to do.

"But you have come to mount Zion, and the city of the Living God, celestial Jerusalem, and ten thousand messengers, to a universal convocation, and to the ecclesia of the *firstborn, registered in the heavens*, and to God, the judge of all, and to the spirits of the just perfected, and to Jesus, the Mediator of a fresh covenant, and to the blood of sprinkling which is speaking better than Abel." (Heb. 12:22-24).

Paul Enters His Ministry

Saul, later called Paul, was still breathing out threatening and murder against disciples of the Lord. Approaching the chief priest, he requested letters for Damascus to the synagogues, that if he should find any along the way, men or women, he may be leading them bound to Jerusalem.

As he neared Damascus, suddenly a light flashed about him. Falling to the earth, he heard a voice saying to him, "Saul, Saul, why are you persecuting Me?" (Acts 9:5). Saul inquired as to Who He was. "I am Jesus Whom you are persecuting. Nevertheless, rise and enter the city, and it will be spoken to you what you must be doing." (Acts 9:5-6).

Saul was to learn he was a choice instrument for Jesus, to bear His name to the nations, (Ephraim), and Kings, and the sons of Israel, the two tribes. He would be intimating to him how much he must suffer for His namesake.

Upon reaching Jerusalem, he tried to join the disciples, but they did not believe he was a disciple and they feared him. Yet Barnabas led him to the apostles and explained his experience on the way to Damascus. Saul spoke boldly in the name of Jesus.

A man named Cornelius, devout and fearing God with his entire house, and had been praying to God continually, was given a vision about the ninth hour of the day. A messenger of God entered to him saying, "Cornelius!" He was frightened, saying, "What is it Lord?" (Acts 10:4). The messenger told him his prayers and his alms had ascended for a memorial to God. He was told to send men to Joppa and ask for a certain Simon, who is surnamed Peter. He would be lodging with a certain Simon, a tanner, whose house was beside the sea. The messengers, two domestics and a devout soldier, after being given instructions, dispatches them to Joppa.

As the three of them neared the city, Peter went upon the housetop to pray. It was about the sixth hour of the day, and Peter became ravenous and wanted something to eat. While they were preparing food for him, the heavens opened and a certain utensil descended, like a large sheet with four edges, was let down upon the earth. On it were all the quadrupeds and reptiles on the earth and flying creatures of the heavens. "Rise Peter! Sacrifice and eat!" (Acts 10:13). Peter said, "Far from me Lord for I never ate anything contaminating and unclean!" The voice came a second time to him. "What God cleanses, do not count contaminating!" (Acts 10:14-16). After occurring three times the utensil was taken up into heaven.

Peter was bewildered as to what the vision should mean. The men dispatched by Cornelius stood at the portal. Peter was engrossed concerning the vision, and a spirit said to him, "Lo three men are seeking you! But, rising, descend and go with them, nothing doubting, for I have commissioned them." (Acts 10:19-20).

On the next day they entered Caesarea. Cornelius was hoping for his people to be accepted by the Jews. (It seems clear that Cornelius was of the ten tribes hoping and praying for the two houses to be reunited). As Cornelius fell at Peter's feet and worshiped him, Peter raises him, saying, "Rise! I also am a man." (Acts 10:27). Then Peter inquires of what the visit is about.

Now Peter begins to speak, saying that of a truth he has grasped that God is not partial, but in every nation the ones that are fearing Him and are acting righteously are acceptable. He says they are aware of the declarations coming down the whole of Judah, beginning at Galilee after the baptism

John heralds.

Now as Peter begins to speak, the holy spirit falls on them even as it did at the beginning. Peter says, "Now I am reminded of the Lord, as He said that John, indeed baptizes in water, yet you shall be baptized in holy spirit!" (Acts 11:16).

For several years, I believed that water baptism was not appropriate for those of the Grace Covenant. Water baptism is a work as is circumcision, and we are not given to works. Then a friend of mine loaned me a book to read. The importance of baptism took up a considerable amount of space. He gave references, even from Paul's writings, to make his point. Sure enough it told of people being baptized. I had based my opinion on verses at Eph. 2:8-10, which reads "For in grace, are you saved, through faith, and this is not out of you, it is God's approach present, not of works, lest anyone should boast." My first thoughts were to admit I was wrong for Paul had certainly said so. I was left in that quandary until I read these words here in Acts. The Lord Himself said, "John [the Baptist] indeed, baptized in water, yet you shall be baptized in holy spirit." That removed works from being a problem.

Perhaps the following from the book of Zechariah will help to distinguish between the two baptisms. Zechariah sees a vision and is asked what he sees. He sees a lampstand, all in gold and a globe at its top, and seven branches, and seven tubes for the lamps which are on top. He sees two olive trees over it, one on the right and one on the left of the globe. Zechariah asks what the two olive limbs are for, by which the golden conduits are emptying the golden oil from above. They are the two sons of clear oil who are standing by. They are Elijah, representing works, and Enoch, representing grace. Now works never saved anyone, nevertheless, in Old Testament times, they were required to carry out works which God established for them to do. Enoch represented grace. It was the grace oil, so to speak, that when mixed with the works oil, became the propitiatory shelter. It was God's faith in the then future shed blood of Christ and His resurrection that saved them. See Zec. 4:1-14.

Note! It seems wise, at this time, to make

the following point clear. I believe it is little wonder that most readers of Scripture are misled by the translations concerning the matter pertaining to the nations. Most of the Versions, I'm aware of, use the term Gentiles, when it should read nations. This error conceals the true meaning that Paul was writing primarily to Ephraim (the ten tribes), and considered them nations. I'm not sure the translators of Scripture are entirely to blame. It may well be that God wanted the truth withheld until the end times. At Zech. 10:8, we read, "I shall hiss for them, and convene them." Could it be that God is making it known now because the end time is near?

Paul Writes to the Ephesians

Having read the book of Ephesians dozens of times, I hadn't noticed the reason for the distinction between use of pronouns in the first fourteen verses of Ephesians. We, us and our, occur thirteen times, denoting the two tribes of Israel, while you and your, designating Ephraim, occurs but three times.

When we realize Paul is speaking of those 10,000 members of the body of Christ, and then remember that Paul was speaking of them in the first twelve verses, and that Paul was of the tribe of Benjamin, we see reason Ephraim is not mentioned until verses thirteen and fourteen. The object is to show the two houses coming together. Here, we will emphasize those pronouns.

"Blessed be the God and Father of *our* Lord Jesus Christ, Who blesses *us* with every spiritual blessing among the celestials, in Christ, according as He chooses *us* in Him before the disruption of the world, *we* to be holy and flawless in His sight, in love designating *us* beforehand for the place of a son for Him through Christ Jesus; in accord with the delight of His will, for the laud of the glory of His grace, which graces *us* in the beloved: in Whom *we* are having the deliverance through His blood, the forgiveness of offenses in accord with the riches of His grace, which He lavishes on *us*; in all wisdom and prudence making known to *us* the secret of His will (in accord with His delight, which He purposed in Him) to have an administration of the complement of the eras, to head up all in Christ, both that in the heavens and that on the earth, in Him in Whom *our* lot was cast also, being *designated beforehand* according to the purpose of the One Who is operating all in accord with the council of His will, that *we* should be for the laud of His glory, *who are pre-expectant in the Christ."* (Eph. 1:3-12).

Then in verses thirteen and fourteen, Paul says, "In Whom *you* also [Ephraim]—on hearing the word of truth, the evangel of *your* salvation—Whom on believing also, *you* are sealed with the holy spirit of promise (which is an earnest of the enjoyment of *our* allotment, to the deliverance of that which has been procured) for the laud of His glory!" (Eph. 1:13-14).

"And *you* [Ephraim] being dead to *your* offenses and sins in which *you* walked, in accord with the eon of this world, in accord with the chief of the jurisdiction of the air, the spirit now operating in the sons of stubbornness (among whom *we* also all behaved once in the lusts of *our* flesh, doing the will of the flesh and of the comprehension, and were, in *our* nature, children of indignation, even as the rest), yet God, being merciful because of His vast love, vivifies us *together* in Christ, and seats us *together* among the celestials in Christ Jesus, that, in the oncoming eons, He should be displaying the transcendence of His kindness to us in Christ Jesus." (Eph. 2:1-7).

Rarely do we see these next two thoughts explained properly. The first is as follows. "For in grace, through faith, are *you* saved, and this is not out of *you*, it is God's approach present, not of works, lest anyone should be boasting." Ephraim is saved by grace, given from God and no works are required. This is because after the resurrection of Christ, the New Covenant was given to Paul to teach to Ephraim. The second thought is as follows. "For His achievement are *we*, being created in Christ Jesus *for good works,* which God makes ready beforehand that *we* should be walking in them." Those of the circumcision were given works to carry out, and then were given God's faith to carry out the works. (Eph. 2:8-10).

Many students of Scripture assume these next verses refer to Gentiles that are alienated, but that cannot be. It was the ten tribe nations that were alienated when they were cast away. They were termed the "Uncircumcision." It was meant as a humiliating term for allowing themselves to be cast away. They were no longer citizens of Israel, only guests of the promise covenants. They no longer had an expectation and were without God in the world. This was always true of Gentiles. They could not be alienated from something they were never a part of. (Eph. 2:11-12).

Now *you* (Ephraim) who were once scattered around the world, have become near by the blood of Christ. He is also peace to those near, and now He tears down the wall of bitterness between them that He might create the two in Himself, into one new humanity, making peace. He is reconciling both in one body to God through the cross, thus destroying the hatred between them. He brings peace to those afar, and peace to those near, for through Christ, both have had access, in one spirit to the Father. (Eph. 2:13-22).

No longer are you scattered ones, guests and sojourners, but are fellow citizens, and belong to God's family. They are built on the foundation of the apostles and prophets, with the corner stone being Christ Jesus. The entire building is connected and growing into a holy temple in the Lord. You are also being built together for God's dwelling place in spirit.

The following are words that seem to be forgotten by so many, yet they could hardly be forgotten, it is more likely they were seen, but it was not known what to do about them. It tells us that all, not only on earth, but *those in the heavens also*, will be saved through the blood of the cross. "And He is the Head of the body, the ecclesia Who is Sovereign, Firstborn from among the dead, that in all He may be becoming first, for in Him the entire complement delights to dwell, and through Him to reconcile *all* to Him *(making peace through the blood of His cross), through Him, whether those on earth or those in the heavens.*" (Col. 1:18-20).

When God created the sovereignties and authorities of the universe, they were created in spirit only. But being of spirit only, the only way they could come to know God was by God's gift of faith. But that would not take care of the sin problem. We can be very sure this did not come as a surprise to God. During the time of chaos and before the eons were established, God chose 144,000 of those celestial beings to become the complement of the eras for an administration to head up all in the Christ, both in the heavens and that on the earth.

At Lev. 17:11 and 14, we read that the soul of the flesh is in the blood, and that the soul of the flesh *is* the blood. I believe this opens the door to understanding a great truth. Since the celestial beings are spirit only, they cannot be forgiven their sins for they have no flesh or blood. Of course, God knew this when He brought them into being. And that's why He made the eons, and why He made His Expression of flesh and blood. So, being both flesh and blood, and the Son of God, Jesus lived the life that it was impossible for any other human to live. That also supplies reason God can now provide salvation by unmerited grace. After living thirty-three years of sinless life, then voluntarily giving His life on the cross: after three days and three nights in the tomb, God raised Him up to heaven to sit on a throne at His right hand.

This is the administration of the secret, which has been concealed from the eons in God. Now it is made known, through Paul, to the sovereignties and authorities among the celestials, through the ecclesia (members of the body or complement of the eras). This was the purpose for the eons and the multifarious wisdom of God, which He made in Christ Jesus our Lord.

So, all humanity is made in the image of a celestial being and is out of the multifarious wisdom of God. Through Jesus Christ, God is bringing salvation to every human being and every celestial being. That was the purpose for the eons. God will not allow one human being to spend eternity in the lake of fire and lose one celestial being.

God's Purpose for the Eons

Paul considers himself to be a prisoner of Christ Jesus for the ten tribe nations. He has written to them before in brief, but he feels they will comprehend his words more clearly now. "In spirit the nations are to be joint enjoyers of an allotment and a joint body, and joint partakers of the promise in Christ Jesus, through the evangel of which I became the dispenser, in accord with the gratuity of the grace of God, which is granted in accord with His powerful operation." (Eph. 3:1-7).

Paul has received a much fuller revelation now, which tells us God's entire objective was for uniting humanity with the sovereignties and authorities. This is that powerful operation. "To me, less than the least of all saints, was granted this grace: to bring the evangel of the untraceable riches of Christ to the nations, and to enlighten all as to what is the administration of the secret, which has been concealed from the eons in God, Who creates all, that now may be made known to the sovereignties and authorities among the celestials, through the ecclesia, the multifarious wisdom of God, in accord with the purpose of the eons, which He makes in Christ Jesus our Lord, in Whom we have boldness and access with confidence, through His faith." (Eph. 3:8-13).

So, God made the eons in Christ Jesus, knowing that the sovereignties and authorities could reach no higher than to live in sin forever, for they could not die. The eons provided for a different atmosphere.

One may well wonder what happens to the sovereignties and authorities since they will be saved. And what are we to say about these Scriptures, found at 1 Cor. 15:24, when He shall be giving the kingdom to His God and Father, whenever He should be *nullifying* all sovereignties and authorities and power.

The purpose of the eons was to bring the evangel of the untraceable riches of Christ to the nations, and to enlighten all as to the meaning of the administration of the secret, the secret that has been concealed in God— the multifarious wisdom of God.

The purpose of God for the eons was

certainly not to bring death to those celestial beings. It was to enlighten them, for what has occurred for man, has really occurred for them, for we are those sovereignties and authorities of the universe. What occurs in us really occurs for them. They will be nullified because they will have become human.

Having become flesh, Jesus redeemed all humanity from their sins. Being God in the flesh, every one of those sovereignties and authorities are also redeemed. This is the powerful operation of God. It is the untraceable riches of Christ. It is the multifarious wisdom of God. It is the most wonderful thing ever to happen to both humanity and to the sovereignties and authorities of the heavens.

When Paul arrived in Rome he was met by the foremost of the Jews, and they said to him: "For, indeed, concerning this sect, it is known to us that everywhere it is being contradicted." (Acts 28:22). Satan has been given far reaching influence over the minds and hearts of men. The "eternal torment doctrine" has been the dominant work of Satan for two thousand years, becoming prevalent in Paul's time, and has done much to distort the truth and confuse the minds of men.

As a result, the evangel of God, which is the evangel of the grace of God, teaching the unmerited salvation of all humanity and built upon the "untraceable riches of Christ," was already giving way to Satan's "doctrine of eternal torment" in Paul's day. I believe the clear message of grace will be brought again in these last days, and when it arrives, the full fury of Satan's wrath shall be unleashed in an attempt to totally destroy the message of grace. Surely that day is rapidly approaching.

In Paul's second letter to Timothy, he tells him to herald the word. Stand by it, opportunely, inopportunely, expose, rebuke, entreat, with all patience and teaching. *"For the era will be when they will not tolerate sound teaching, but, their hearing being tickled, they will heap for themselves teachers in accord with their own desires, and indeed, they will be turning their hearing away from the truth and will be turned aside to myths."* (11 Tim. 4.3-4)

The Evangel of God or The New Covenant

Paul begins this subject to the Corinthians with the following words. "Are we beginning again to commend ourselves? Or need we not, even as some, commendatory letters to you from us?" (11 Cor. 3:1). He says the *people* are their letter engraved on their hearts and read by all men. They are manifesting a letter of Christ, dispensed by Paul and the evangelists with him, and engraved not with ink, but with the spirit of their God. Not on stone tablets, but on the fleshly tablets of the heart. This is the confidence they have in Christ Jesus toward God, and not of themselves, for their competency is of God. It is God Who makes them competent of a New Covenant, not of the letter, but of the spirit. The letter kills, but the spirit vivifies.

Moses placed a covering over his face so the sons of Israel could not look intently to the consummation of that which was being nullified. But what they expected was calloused, for to this very day that same covering remains at the reading of the Old Covenant. It was only uncovered when Christ nullified it.

Now the words bringing death, chiseled in stone, came in glory. The sons of Israel could not look intently into the face of Moses because of the glory shown on his face, which is being nullified. How much rather, the dispensation of righteousness exceeds it in glory. Now if that which is being nullified was nullified through glory, much rather that which is remaining, remains in glory.

The expression, "the evangel of God," occurs a total of eight or nine times in the letters of Paul. Four of those occurrences are found in the first two chapters of First Thessalonians. That is understandable when we consider it being the first letter of his writings. This letter is from Paul, Silvanus and Timothy, and was written soon after their visit.

Since that visit they have prayed to Jesus Christ constantly remembering their work of faith, and toil, and love, and endurance in expectation of the Lord Jesus Christ. Before God the Father, they perceived their choice for the evangel of their God. It came with power also, and of the holy spirit and much assurance as the people were aware.

The Thessalonians became imitators of the ecclesia in Judea in Christ Jesus. They had suffered by the Jews, just as those in Judea suffered by them. They even killed the Lord Jesus Christ and the prophets. Now the Jews have even banished Paul and his ministers, forbidding them from speaking to the nations that they should be saved, thus filling up their own sins.

Now Paul and his fellow evangelists have been driven out of Thessalonia, in face, but not in heart. They had wanted to return but Satan prevented them. They had reached Athens when Paul could no longer refrain. They sent Timothy back as God's servant in the evangel of Christ. He was fearful his toil had been in vain. Timothy returned with good news that those people have great remembrance of their ministry. They longed to see Paul even as Paul longed to see them.

The matter we should learn from this, is that the evangel of God does not replace the evangel of Christ, The evangel of God is built upon the evangel of Christ. The marvelous truth is that all humanity is being saved by grace. And that is what the New Covenant is about.

The Salvation of all (Rev. 15:20-28)

"Through a man came death, through a man, also, comes the resurrection of the dead. For even as, in Adam, *all* are dying, thus also, in Christ, *all* shall be vivified." (1 Cor. 15:21-22). Now, the equality of the two could hardly be made plainer. To say [just as] in place of (even as), might be clearer, but it would not change the meaning. We read that the salvation of all humanity is broken down into three groups. We know that Christ is the Firstfruit of all to be raised from death. But the word firstfruit, is one of those words that may be either singular or plural. The first group are those making up the body of Christ and are the firstfruit, plural. (See Rev. 14: 3B-5). The second group are those who are His at His coming, at the end of the tribulation period. The third group to be saved is at the consummation, whenever Christ may be giving up the kingdom to His God and Father, whenever He should be nullifying all authority and power. He must be reigning until He places *all* enemies under His feet. *"The last enemy is being abolished: death."* (See 1 Cor.15:24-28. And that will occur at the consummation, when those corruptible ones, in the lake of fire, shall put on incorruption.

These verses say those celestial beings are legally made null and void. The meaning is to do away with their present purpose. They lose their sovereignty and present authority. That is because they become human and transformed into a new celestial being.

Here Paul reveals a secret. "We shall not *all* die, yet *all* shall be changed, in the twinkle of an eye, at the last trump. God will be trumpeting, and the dead will be roused incorruptible, and all will be changed, for the corruptible must put on incorruption and this mortal put on immortality. Now whenever this corruptible should be putting on incorruption, and this mortal should be putting on immortality, then shall come to

pass the word which is written.
Swallowed up was Death by Victory.
Where, O Death, is your victory?
Where, O Death, is your sting?"
(1Cor.15:50-55).

God's Secret: The Tiny Scroll

John perceived another strong messenger coming down from heaven, clothed in a cloud, and a rainbow on its head. His face was as the sun, and his feet as pillars of fire. In his hand was a tiny open scroll. He places his right foot on the sea, and his left foot on the land. He cries with a loud voice, as a lion bellowing.

When he cries, the seven thunders speak with their own voices. And when they spoke, John was about to write when he heard a voice out of heaven saying, "Seal what things the seven thunders speak, and those you should not be writing." (Rev. 10:4).

The messenger, with his feet upon the land and on the sea, lifts his right hand to heaven and swears by Him Who is living for the eons of the eons, Who created heaven and earth and the sea, that there will no longer be time to delay. In the days of the seventh messenger's voice, whenever he may be about to trumpet, the secret of God is consummated also, as he evangelizes to His Own slaves and prophets. And the voice which John heard, speaks again to him saying, "Go get the tiny scroll open in the hands of the messenger standing on the sea and on the land." (Rev. 10:8). John went to the messenger asking for the tiny scroll. The messenger said to him, "Take it and devour it, and it will make your bowels bitter, but in your mouth, it will be sweet as honey." (Rev. 10:9). And John took the tiny scroll out of the messenger's hand and devoured it. And in his mouth, it was sweet as honey. And when he ate it his bowels were made bitter. And they were saying to him, "You must prophesy again over peoples and nations and languages and many kings." (Rev. 10:11).

The secret of God was contained in the tiny scroll. The reason it was sweet as honey in John's mouth was because all the names of Ephraim were there, and they would be protected from the last half of the tribulation when they would be taken into the wilderness for protection from its horrors. The reason it was bitter in his bowels was because the names of the two tribes were not there, and they would be required to face those horrors by going through the tribulation.

Two Great Signs Seen in Heaven (Rev. 12:1-17)

A great sign was seen in heaven. A woman was seen clothed with the sun. The moon was under her feet, and on her head was a wreath of twelve stars. She was pregnant and crying and tormented to bring forth her child. The sun represents the greater glory of Ephraim, while the moon represents the lesser glory of Manasseh.

Another sign was seen in heaven. A fiery red dragon, having seven heads and ten horns, and seven diadems on its head. It's tail is dragging one third of the stars of heaven, and casts them to the earth. The dragon stands before the woman who is about to bear her child, to devour it whenever she gives birth. She brings forth a son who is about to shepherd all the nations with an iron club. The child is snatched away to God.

The woman (the Ephraim aspect) flees into the wilderness where she shall be nourished for a thousand two hundred and sixty days. This is the number of days in the final half of the tribulation.

The great dragon was cast into the earth, and its messengers with it. John heard a loud voice saying, "Just now came the salvation and the power and the kingdom of our God, and the authority of His Christ, for the accuser of our brethren was cast out, who was accusing them before God, day and night. And they conquer him through the blood of the Lambkin, and through the word of His testimony, and they love not their soul, unto death."(Rev. 12:10-11).

When the serpent is cast to the earth, it persecutes the woman that brought forth the male child. Given to the woman were two wings of a large vulture, that she will be nourished a season, seasons, and half a season from the face of the serpent. The dragon casts water as a river out of its mouth that the woman should be carried away. The earth swallowed the water to help the woman. The serpent is angry and goes away to battle with the rest of her seed. This would be the two-tribe people that will enter the tribulation horrors.

Seven Letters to Seven Ecclesias

John came to be in spirit when he heard a voice, loud as a trumpet saying, "What you are observing, write in a scroll and send it to the seven ecclesias: To Ephesus and to Smyrna and to Pergamum and to Thyatira and to Sardis and to Philadelphia and to Laodicea." (Rev. 1:11).

He turned to look where the voice was coming from, and he observed seven golden lampstands. In their midst he saw One like a son of mankind, dressed in a garment reaching to His feet. His breasts are wrapped with a golden girdle. His head and hair are white as snow, as wool. His eyes are as a flame of fire. His feet are like white bronze, as fired in a furnace, and a voice as the sound of many waters. In His right hand are seven stars. Out of His mouth is issuing a sharp two-edged blade. His appearance is as the sun in its power.

When John perceived this One, he fell to His feet as dead. He placed His right hand upon John and said, "Do not fear! I am the First and the Last, and the Living One: and I became dead, and Lo! Living am I for the eons of the eons. (Amen!) And I have the keys of death and the unseen. Write then what you have seen, and what they are, and what is about to be occurring, after these things: the secret of the seven stars which you perceived in My right hand, and the seven golden lampstands. The seven stars are the messengers of the seven ecclesias, and the seven lampstands are the seven ecclesias." (Rev. 1:18-20).

The people making up these ecclesias are those of Ephraim (the ten lost tribes), each consisting of a period of time according to the order in which the letters were written. It is the Lord Jesus Christ that tells John what to write in each of the letters to the messengers. It is the messenger that delivers the message when the people become located in their respective ecclesia. Every letter begins by informing the people that He is aware of how they conducted themselves, good or bad. Every letter ends with these words: "Who has an ear, let him hear what the spirit is saying to the ecclesia."

The first message is to the ecclesia of Ephesus. The Lord is aware of their toil and endurance, and that they cannot bear evil men, and they try those who say they are prophets, and are not. They found those to be false. They have endured and bear the name and are not wearied. But they left their first love. They allowed themselves to be cast away. They must remember why they fell and repent as before. If not, He will come and remove their lampstand. One thing pleases Him. They hate the Nicolaitans, even as He hates them. (Probably as worshippers of Satan).

"Who has an ear, let him hear what the spirit is saying to the ecclesia."

The second message is to the ecclesia of Smyrna. It is from the One Who is the First and the Last, Who became dead, and lives. He is aware of their acts and affliction and poverty (but they are rich) and are falsely saying they are Jews, but are not, but are a synagogue of Satan. Do not fear what you are about to suffer. Satan is about to cast some of them into jail to try them with affliction for ten days. Become faithful until death, and He will give them a wreath of life. To the one who is conquering, he will under no circumstances be injured by the second death.

"Who has an ear, let him hear what the spirit is saying to the ecclesia."

The third message is to the ecclesia of Pergamum. The one speaking to John is the One Who has the sharp two-edged blade. He is aware of where they are dwelling, where the throne of Satan is, and they hold Jesus' name, and do not disown His faith in the days in which Antipas, His faithful witness, was killed among them, where Satan is dwelling. But He has a few things against them. Some of them hold to the teaching of Baalam. He taught Balak to cast a snare before the sons of Israel, to eat idol sacrifices, and commit prostitution. They also have those believing the teachings of the Nicolaitans. Repent then! But if not, He is coming swiftly to battle with the blade of His mouth. He will be giving hidden manna to those conquering, and He will give them a white pebble, and on it shall be written a new name. No one will be aware of the name except the one receiving it.

"Who has an ear, let him hear what the spirit is saying to the ecclesia."

The fourth message is to the ecclesia of Thyatira. The Son of God speaks to them, Who's eyes are as a flame of fire, and feet like white bronze. He is aware of their acts and love and faith and service and endurance, and their last acts are more than the former. But He has much against them, seeing that they pardon that woman, Jezebel, who claims to be a prophetess, but is teaching and deceiving His slaves to commit prostitution and to be eating idol sacrifices. He gives her time to repent, but she is not willing to repent of her prostitution. Lo! He will cast her into a couch, and those committing adultery with her, into great affliction. If they will not be repenting of her acts, He shall be killing them with death. All the ecclesias will know that it is He Who searches the kidneys and hearts. He will give to each in accord with their acts. Now to the rest in Thyatira, whoever does not have this teaching, (does not know the deep things of Satan), He will cast no other burden upon them. Moreover, hold what you have until He arrives. To the one conquering and keeping His acts until the end, He will give authority over the nations; and he shall shepherd them with an iron club, as vessels of pottery being crushed, as I obtained from My Father. And I will give him the morning star.

"Who has an ear, let him hear what the spirit is saying to the ecclesias."

The fifth message is to the ecclesia of Sardis. John writes to the messenger as from the One Who has the seven spirits of God and the seven stars. Jesus is aware of their acts. They have a name that they are living, but they are dead. Be watchful and establish the rest, who are about to die, for He does not find their acts completed in the sight of God. They must remember how they obtained and hear. Keep it and repent. If they should not be watching, He will arrive as a thief. Under no circumstances will they know the hour of His arrival. But you in Sardis have a few who do not pollute their garments. They shall walk with Him in white, for they are worthy.

The one who conquers shall be clothed in white. By no means will He erase their name from the scroll of life. He will avow their name in front of His Father, and before His messenger.

"Who has an ear, let him hear what the spirit is saying to the ecclesia."

Not having knowledge of the history of those some 2600 years that Ephraim (the ten lost tribes) has been scattered throughout the world, and were not God's people, a good guess seems to be that the time of Philadelphia, probably began with the reformation and ended with the second world war. It seems clear that with the reformation came the formation of many denominations, and a closer relationship with God. Having grown up during the depression, I notice a great change following, and it was toward that indifference. Laodicea then would follow until the arrival of the tribulation.

The sixth message is to the ecclesia of Philadelphia. This is from the True and Holy One Who has the key of David and Who opens, and no one shall be locking, and locking and no one shall be opening.

"I am aware of your acts." Before you, He has granted an open door, which no one is able to lock, for you have some power, and you keep His word and do not disown His name. But He has granted to those of the synagogue of Satan, those who say they are Jews, but are not, and are lying, to make them arrive and worship at Your feet, that you may know that He loves you. Since they keep the word of His endurance, He will keep them out of the hour of trial, which is about to come upon the whole inhabited earth. He is coming swiftly. Hold on to what you have, that no one takes your wreath.

The one who conquers, He will make a pillar in the temple of His God, that He may not be coming out. He will write on him the name of His God, and the name of the city of His God, the new Jerusalem, which is descending out of heaven from His God, and His new name.

"Who has an ear, let him hear what the

spirit is saying to the ecclesia."

The seventh message is to the ecclesia of Laodicea. These are sayings of the Amen! the Faithful and True Witness, and God's creative original.

"I am aware of your acts." Neither cool are you nor zealous! He would rather they were one or the other: but seeing their indifference, He will spew them out of His mouth. They say they are rich, and rich have I become, and they have need of nothing! They are not aware that they are wretched and forlorn and poor and blind and naked. He advises them to buy of Him gold refined in the fire, and they will become rich, and buy garments that they may be clothed, and the shame of their nakedness be made manifest, and eye-salve to anoint their eyes, that they may be observing.

Whoever He may be fond of, He is exposing and disciplining. So be zealous and repent. He stands at the door and is knocking. If anyone hears His voice and opens the door, He will come in and dine with them and they with Him.

To the one conquering, to them will He grant a seat with Him on His throne.

"Who has an ear, let him hear what the spirit is saying to the ecclesia."

All Ephraim is Saved by Grace

John perceived a messenger ascending from the orient, having the seal of the living God. He heard the number of those to be sealed as 144,000. Twelve thousand out of each tribe of Israel. They are Judah, Reuben, Gad, Asher, Naphtali, Manasseh, Simeon, Levi, Issachar, Zebulon, Joseph and Benjamin.

After the 144,000 were given seals on their foreheads, John perceived a vast throng which no one was able to number, out of every nation (from wherever they were scattered) and out of every tribe and peoples and languages, standing before the throne and the Lambkin, clothed in white robes and with palm fronds in their hands. This is probably billions, making up those of Ephraim.

All the messengers and the twenty-four elders and the four animals stood around the throne. They fall on their faces and worship

God, saying, "Amen! Blessing and glory and wisdom, and thanks and honor, and power and strength be our God's for the eons of the eons. Amen!" (Rev. 7:11-12).

"These are those coming out of the great affliction, [thus avoiding its horror's]. And they rinse their robes, and they whiten them in the blood of the Lambkin. *Therefore,* they are before the throne of God, and are offering divine service to Him day and night in his temple. And He Who is sitting on the throne will be tabernacling over them. They shall not be hungering longer, nor shall they be thirsting any longer: no, neither shall the sun be falling on them, nor any heat, seeing that the throne-centered Lambkin shall be shepherding over them, and shall be guiding them to living springs of water, and every tear shall God be brushing away from their eyes." (Rev. 7:14-17). All Ephraim has found salvation.

As for Manasseh, the two tribes, see our study at Isa. 49:13-26. They shall follow soon after Ephraim. And we read the following at Rom. 11:25-27.

"For I am not willing for you to be ignorant of this secret, brethren, lest you may be passing for prudent among yourselves, that callousness, in part, on Israel has come, until the complement of the nations may be entering. And thus, all Israel may be saved, according as it is written, arriving out of Zion shall be the Rescuer. He will be turning irreverence from Jacob. And this is My covenant with them whenever I should be eliminating their sins." (Roms. 11:25-27). Great are the plans and purposes of God.

A BRIEF STUDY OF THE EONS

The misuse of two words found within the pages of the Authorized Version of the Holy Scriptures, have done more to create havoc in arriving at a proper understanding of the Scriptures than any other error. It has allowed the apostasy of Satan to gain its strong foothold in virtually every denomination of the protestant churches, by bringing forth the "eternal torment doctrine." These words are "olam," from the Hebrew Writings, and "aion" from the Greek. While it is not our desire at this time to delve into the confusion caused by the English translations of the Hebrew word, olam, we do wish to list some of those occurrences. We recognize the difficulty in overcoming traditional views cast upon us by ones already set in those traditions. We ask that each reader begin these pages prayerfully, and with an open mind in hopes of reaching new and marvelous depths of understanding of the Scriptures.

The word, olam occurs 448 times in the Authorized Version of the Old Testament writings, and is given at least 25 different English meanings. In 246 occurrences it is rendered, forever; in 11 occurrences it is rendered, ever; and in 19 occurrences it is rendered, forever and ever. In 15 contexts the word is stated as, for evermore; 13 contexts have it as, of old, or ever of old, 56 contexts state it as, everlasting; and it is rendered as perpetual in 22 contexts. In addition to these it is translated as anymore, long, world, continuance, eternal, lasting, long time, at any time, since the beginning of the world, and still others. The English words "ever and ever" seem to indicate the plural form of the word. That alone destroys their concept of the meaning by suggesting one eternity is followed by another eternity. In almost every one of the 448 instances, the contexts clearly indicate involvement of the element of time. And every occurrence was translated from the Hebrew term "olam."

Without doubt the most enlightening discovery in my years of Bible Study came nearly fifty-five years ago when a dear friend, Elwood Gustafson, introduced me to this study designed to clarify the true meaning of those words. We know of several writers having done work on the subject: Leon A. Bynoe's The Eonian Times; The Ages in the Scriptures, by Vladimir Gelesnoff; Grace H. Todd's Eonian-Everlasting or Age-lasting; and indeed much writing on the subject by A.E. Knoch. The common consensus of these writers is that the eons are but a relatively brief interval of time, but placed within an immeasurable expanse: that expanse having no definite beginning and no end. Though the eons are as a brief moment compared with eternity, probably more than 95% of Scripture deals with that time period.

It is the New Testament Scriptures of which we are most concerned in this study. The nearest English equivalent to the Greek word aion is age, and simply denotes a period of time. It is often used in plural, showing that more than one eon is involved. The Concordant Publishers of the Scriptures have considered it to be more Scriptural to use the original, since it works no hardship to the English text. This has been done with many Latin words finding their way into the English language. However, the spelling has customized aion and aions so they become eon and eons. Eon is the noun, while eonian is the adjective describing the noun. And incidentally the adjective has created as much havoc as the noun. Henceforth we shall use the terms eon and eonian.

Leon A. Bynoe gives us a brief history describing the loss of value for this word. Eonian Times was a well-founded Scriptural term, but it became lost, and the truth concerning it became obscured. Its collapse left the way for pagan error to enter. This occurred quickly after the time of the apostle Paul. Mr. Bynoe says it appears only a few scholars have said much about this term after Paul's time, allowing for a few exceptions, until much later. The historian used it at the end of the second century AD; Lactanius, born about AD 265, Eusebius, an early church historian, born about AD 225, and Wyclif, born about 1320, also used the term. Bynoe says the record shows that the

Latin fathers, led by Jerome, who gave us the Latin Vulgate Version, began the departure from the original. In the year 696 at Constantinople, a council of the Roman Church publicly condemned the doctrine of the eons. Apparently this was done in support of Origen's stand, which called it "Drunken ravings of the future of the dead." In 1470, Tyndale brought in the totally false teaching of endlessness, adding words such as eternal, forever and ever, and everlasting: all of these supposedly describing the Greek root word meaning aion—a period of time.

The revival for the use of the word aion, Bynoe says, did not come by the advent of the Concordant Version. The emphatic Diaglott had already used it: rendering it consistently as "ages." Other good version rendered it as ages: American Revised, Darby, Rotherham, Moffatt and Goodspeed.

Leon Bynoe quotes Clarence Larkin concerning the following thoughts. The Greek word, "aion" meaning age, has been translated in the Authorized Version by eight different English words: ages, twice; ever, 30 times; ever and ever 21 times; world, 35 times; worlds, twice; course, once;

eternal, twice; and end, once. When the word "age" is used it will be seen that a period of time is in view: rather than the material world. He shows we have a singular eon. At Mat. 24:3; the plural eons, at Eph. 2:7; at Rev. 20:10, both are plural, as eons of the eons; and one singular and one plural, as eon of the eons at Eph.3:11.

The Greek-English Lexicons usually define "olam" in the Hebrew, and "aion" in the Greek, Bynoe says, as an indefinite period of time similar to an age. The difficulty caused by the translators of the AV or KJV is, they have stretched the meaning to include forever, evermore, eternal, everlasting, forever and ever, always, world, eternity, and world without end: always having the idea of endlessness in mind. This author asks, "How could it be possible for one Greek word to cover so many different terms in the English Bibles? Then the fault lies with the clergy, and neither is the layman absolved, because the injunction is to 'search the Scriptures'— correctly partition the truth.'

This of course is much what they did with the word olam of the Hebrew Scriptures.

Old English versions were made from the Latin Vulgate and not from Greek Writings. This was done between AD 680 and AD 995. Bynoe says John Wyclif was probably the first man to translate the entire Bible into the English tongue. He was born in 1320, began translating in 1356, and finished his work in 1382, just two years before he died. He was a great scholar and bitterly opposed the Roman Catholic claims.

While at the University of Prague, John Huss came under the influence of Wyclif. He was burned at the stake in 1415 for his stand of faith. The Latin Vulgate dominated Europe until the time of Wyclif. No one had thought of translating from the Greek scrolls, probably because Latin had taken its place as the universal language. Wyclif remained true to the original Greek. Just one hundred fifty years later, Tyndale led a group of translators *from the original*, following Jerome and the Latin Vulgate. Followed by this were Coverdale's Version (1535), Crammer's (1539), the Genevan (1557), Rheims (1582), and finally the Authorized Version of (1611).

It was Tyndale that caused the Scriptures

to become corrupt with the clouded meaning of the terms. This corruption included many words treated in like manner: we are dealing with but two words. But while the Greek Church declined, the Latin Church rose to prominence. The reformation should have righted us to a correct version of the Greek Scriptures, but instead only reformed along certain lines, and actually confirmed and solidly reestablished the dogmas of the Roman Church. In spite of better versions coming along since the Authorized Version, the masses continue to revere its pages, neglecting the obscured truths hidden in them. That version is not a translation: simply a revision of the Latin Vulgate, and authorized by the king of England.

The word eon means a period of time between two great physical and moral cataclysmic changes of the earth and its inhabitants. There will have been at least four such changes taking place during this total period we consider "eonian times."

Before eonian times; There is Scripture telling us the eons had a beginning. 1 Cor. 2:7 states, wisdom is not of this eon, and what God designates "before the eons" has been concealed from men until now. The body of Christ is told at 11 Tim. 1:9, their calling was given to them in Christ Jesus "before eonian times." Paul tells those of the body at Titus 1:2, they were promised eonian life "before times eonian." (We are not told how long the eons had occurred or how many occurred before the disruption. This study recognizes only that there was at least one eon.)

The first eon: The beginning of the eons is mentioned in John 1:1, where we are told the word already existed at the beginning. All things (eonian) came into being through the word, and in it was life , and the life was the light of men. In Jesus' prayer to the heavenly Father, He acknowledged the Father as loving Him before the "disruption of the world:" this is found at John 17:24. We are told at 1 Peter 1:20, the unspotted Lamb was foreknown before the "disruption"—of the world," and we find the first eon ending with that "disruption" before the six-days of Genesis, chapter one.

The second eon: The beginning of this eon corresponds with the disruption shown in the above paragraph. "Yet the earth became a chaos and vacant and darkness was on the surface of the submerged chaos" (Gen. 1:2). Speaking of the heavens and earth of old cohering out of water and through water, Peter says, "...Through which the then world, being deluged by water, perished" (11 Peter 3:6). The days of Noah marked the end of this second eon, which is bounded by the disruption and the deluge. The deluge is dealt with at Genesis, chapter 6, and at 11 Peter 2:5. Notice this second eon is also called the "then world," as opposed to this current world, suggesting the eons and the worlds correspond with one another.

The third eon: This is called the "present wicked eon" at Gal. 1:4: "...That He [the Lord Jesus Christ] might extricate us out of the present wicked eon." At Luke 21:24 it is referred to as the time when, "...Jerusalem shall be trodden by the nations [this current 2,000 years], until the eras of the nations shall be fulfilled." Then shall come the time of the end (see Mat. 25:31, and Dan. 12:3). The deluge of Noah's time and the end of the great tribulation/coming of Christ to set up His kingdom, provide the boundaries for this eon. At Eph. 2:2 we learn of all sinners having once walked "...In accord with the eon of this world..." Again the eon is synchronized with this present world.

The fourth eon: The millennium and time of regeneration. Matthew makes reference to this eon at Mat. 12:32, "...Yet whoever may be saying aught against the Holy Spirit, it shall not be pardoned him, neither in this eon nor in that which is impending." There it is referred to as the impending eon. (The so-called unpardonable sin is only unpardonable during the eonian times; not for eternity.) We learn that when the thousand years are finished, Satan will be loosed from his jail and will determine to deceive all the nations of the earth. This will mark the end of the fourth eon and the beginning of the fifth, which is the time of the Great White Throne judgment.

The fifth eon: The Great White Throne judgment ushers in the fifth eon, corresponding with the new heaven and new earth. It is the period in which all the unsaved of the eons are cast into the "lake of fire" to undergo suffering and anguish, while their consciences are being perfected. When they cry out for the "living water" they also shall be washed clean. This is the time for reconciliation and perfection of all things. Col. 1:18-20 reveals just how perfect it shall be. "And He [Christ] is the head of the body, the ecclesia, Who is sovereign, Firstborn from among the dead, that in all He may be becoming first, for in Him the entire complement delights to dwell, and through Him to reconcile all to Him (making peace through the blood of His cross), through Him, whether those on the earth or those in the heavens."

The consummation of the eons: It is at this time "death" is abolished. "For He must be reigning until He should be placing all His enemies under His feet. The last enemy is being abolished: death [dying state]. For He subjects all under His feet...that God may be All in all (1 Cor. 15:25-27). And at 1 Cor. 15:54-55 we read the following quotation. "Now, whenever this corruptible should be putting on incorruption and this mortal should be putting on immortality, then shall come to pass the word which is written,

Swallowed up was Death by victory.
Where, O Death, is your victory?
Where, O Death, is your sting?

The following is a tribulation to A.E. Knoch, written by Elder A. Benta

"You will never know how much of the meaning of God's word is hid from you until you understand the subject of the eons. It is one of the key words of Scripture that has been hid from view through mistranslation. God's grand and glorious purpose will never be understood until we learn that the Greek word "aion" transliterated "eon" by the (Concordant Version), is a *time* word. That is to say, it does not denote endlessness as it is so often rendered in our common versions: ever, forever and ever, and world without end. Likewise its adjective is translated everlasting and eternal. These are wholly mistranslations that hide the truth from the vernacular student.

www.ingramcontent.com/pod-product-compliance
Lightning Source LLC
Chambersburg PA
CBHW071926020426
42331CB00010B/2743

* 9 7 8 1 9 6 0 4 9 9 6 8 4 *